D0518362

EDGE
BOOKS™

Prepare to Survive

How to Survive on a
DESERTED ISLAND

by Tim O'Shei

Consultant: Al Siebert, PhD
Author of *The Survivor Personality*

Capstone
press®
Mankato, Minnesota

Edge Books are published by Capstone Press,
151 Good Counsel Drive, P.O. Box 669, Mankato, Minnesota 56002.
www.capstonepress.com

Library of Congress Cataloging-in-Publication Data
O'Shei, Tim.
    How to survive on a deserted island / by Tim O'Shei.
    p. cm. — (Edge books. Prepare to Survive)
    Includes bibliographical references and index.
    ISBN-13: 978-1-4296-2282-0 (hardcover)
    ISBN-10: 1-4296-2282-2 (hardcover)
    1. Wilderness survival — Juvenile literature. 2. Survival after airplane accidents,
shipwrecks, etc. — Juvenile literature. I. Title.
GV200.5.O846 2009
613.6'9 — dc22   2008034521

Summary: Describes tips on how to survive on a deserted island.

Editorial Credits

Angie Kaelberer, editor; Veronica Bianchini, designer; Wanda Winch,
    photo researcher; Sarah L. Schuette, photo stylist; Marcy Morin,
    photo shoot scheduler

Photo Credits

Capstone Press/Gary Sundermeyer, 18 (all); Karon Dubke, 17, 20
Courtesy of Fred Hargesheimer, 11
Getty Images Inc./CBS Photo Archive/Bill Inoshita, 23; Riser/Candela
    Foto Art/Kreuziger, 8–9; Taxi/Alexander Walter, 19
iStockphoto/Jacom Stephens, 5 (inset); Lya Cattel, 4–5; Ziella Marie Chua, 27
Minden Pictures/Christian Ziegler, 15
Rod Whigham, 13, 21, 25
Shutterstock/Alexander Shalamov, 6; Dusan Zidar, front cover; IntraClique, 12;
    Lora Liu, back cover; Mushakesa, 14; Near and Far Photography, 29;
    Willem Tims, 22

1 2 3 4 5 6 14 13 12 11 10 09

Table of Contents

Chapter 1

LANDING ON LAND

The thought of a tropical island usually makes people smile. Gentle ocean waves lapping against a sandy beach. Tall palm trees that dance in the wind and offer shade from a golden sun.

Sounds like a vacation, doesn't it? But islands can also be the sites of life-and-death struggles against nature. On a deserted island, you're surrounded by water. There's no easy way out, and no one is there to help you. Your survival depends on you.

THIS IS NO VACATION!

Surviving on an island can be quite a challenge. The hot sun can burn your skin and make you thirsty. You might think that because there's plenty of water nearby, thirst isn't an issue. But the water is probably saltwater. That means drinking it will only make you thirstier — and possibly kill you.

What about those thick, green plants and trees? Well, yes, they can help you by providing food and shelter. But behind the bushes and underneath the rocks lurk some creepy-crawly bugs and animals. Some of them will become an easy meal. Others, however, may prefer to make a meal out of you. It's all part of the struggle to survive.

Chapter 2

SURVIVING THE ISLAND LIFE

In many survival situations, you run the risk of dying of heat, cold, or starvation. But if you use your brain, you can survive on an island for a long time.

Explore your surroundings. People may have lived on the island before and left useful things behind. Also, look for objects that wash up on the beach. You'll be surprised at how you can use these objects to survive.

THINK LIKE A SURVIVOR

Survival experts say that your top tool for staying alive is your mind. If you think you can survive a scary situation, then there's a better chance you will.

To survive, you have to change your sense of what is comfortable. Realize it's OK to sleep on the ground, even though you want a bed. You might not like fish, but if eating one is what you need to do to survive, then do it! You may become depressed because you miss your family and friends. But remember that you'll only see them again if you live.

MAKE YOURSELF AT HOME

You'll need shelter to protect yourself from the weather. Temperatures on islands are often very hot. Storms form over the ocean and pummel the land with heavy rain.

Consider your choices. Are there any shelters already built, like an abandoned hut or cabin? Are there any caves nearby? Check out these places first. But be careful that it's not already the home of a wild animal!

TIP: Whether you find or build your shelter, make sure it's at least 100 feet (30 meters) from shore. If it's closer, high tide will wash your home out to the ocean.

FRED HARGESHEIMER

It was June 5, 1943. The United States was fighting in World War II (1939-1945). U.S. pilot Fred Hargesheimer was flying over the southwest Pacific Ocean when a Japanese plane fired at him. Hargesheimer parachuted from his burning plane. He landed on the small island of New Britain.

For 10 days, Hargesheimer wandered alone. His only food was two chocolate bars. Eventually, he found an abandoned shelter. He set up camp there and lived on snails after the chocolate ran out.

After a month, local people found Hargesheimer and took him to their village. They hid him from the Japanese for the next seven months. In February 1944, a U.S. Navy crew rescued Hargesheimer. Hargesheimer was so grateful to the villagers that he returned years later to thank them. He also raised money to build a school, library, and clinic on the island.

Fred Hargesheimer (right) survived alone on a Pacific island for more than a month.

How to

BUILD AN ISLAND HOME

If there aren't any shelters awaiting you, you'll have to make your own. Here's how:

1. Find a safe spot. Look for a place in the shade, but be careful. You don't want a coconut or large branch to hit you on the head! Avoid slopes. Rocks and dirt can fall in a landslide, taking your shelter with them.

2. Gather materials. Sturdy tree branches and sticks provide the perfect frame. String, shoelaces, or strong vines can hold your frame together. A **tarp** or rain poncho makes a nice waterproof wall or ceiling. Thick brush can be **insulation**.

3. Lean pairs of sticks together to form a row of triangle shapes, using the ground as your floor. Tie each stick set together with string or vines. Tie a long, polelike stick across the top of several of the triangles to form a wall. Then repeat that step until you have four walls. Tie the walls together to form a square frame.

tarp – a heavy, waterproof covering
insulation – a material that stops heat, sound, or cold from entering or escaping

If you have a tarp or poncho, stretch it across the frame to keep the inside of the shelter dry. If you don't have a tarp, use tall grass and brush. Place large rocks along the base of your shelter. They will help keep the frame and walls in place.

A platform shelter keeps you off the wet, cold ground and away from snakes and crawling bugs. Build this shelter with four tall poles that form a square frame. Lay poles or small logs across the frame to form a platform. Fasten the platform to the frame so it is several feet off the ground.

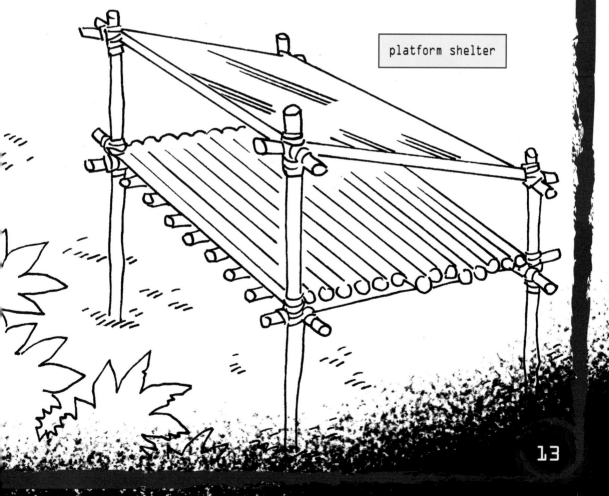

platform shelter

How to

LOCATE WATER

You can survive for weeks without food, but only a few days without water. On an island, rain is often the best source of drinking water. Gather objects that can catch rainwater, such as large seashells or empty turtle shells.

If you're lucky, your island will have a running stream. Just make sure to drink upstream from where you wash. That way, you'll avoid swallowing the germs you scrubbed off your body.

An ant colony can lead
you to a water source.

As you hunt for water, animal trails are your best clue.
If you see tracks, follow them. Even small bugs like ants need
water. If you find an ant colony, water is probably nearby.

A plant growing in an unlikely place, such as a rocky cliff,
can also lead you to water. Beneath the rocks, there's probably
a spring of water feeding the plant's roots.

SOLAR STILLS

It is possible to turn saltwater into fresh water. A solar still uses sunlight to **evaporate** saltwater. You can make a solar still out of a waterproof container and a piece of glass, clear plastic, or plastic wrap. You may be able to find these items in the wreckage of your boat or washed up on the beach.

Place a cup of saltwater inside the solar still and cover the still with the plastic or glass lid. Put a rock on top of the lid to keep it from blowing off. As the sun's rays beat through the lid, the water evaporates. The salt is left in the cup. Drinkable water **condenses** on the lid and runs down the inside of the container.

evaporate — to change from a liquid to a gas
condense — to change from a gas to a liquid

If you don't have a solar still, use the tips on pages 18 and 19 to build a fire. Pour saltwater into a pot and bring it to a boil. Hold a rag or cloth over the pot to soak up the steam. Suck on the rag or wring it into your mouth to get a few sips of clean water.

What if there is no rain, no stream, and you have no way of converting saltwater? You still have options. Dew often forms on leaves and grass in the morning. Wrap cloth on your hands and feet and walk through the wet plants, soaking up the water into the cloth. You can also try digging deep into a dry stream bed. Water often runs underneath. Or if you have a plastic bag, tie it tightly around a tree branch with leaves. Water will condense from the leaves into the bag.

TIP: Never drink saltwater. Your body will use the fluids already inside you to flush out the salt. Plus, drinking saltwater will cause you to get sick and dizzy.

How to

BUILD A FIRE

Fire is incredibly useful for survival. You can use it to cook, keep warm, and boil water.

Find a safe spot for the fire. You'll need a dry place that is clear of low-hanging tree branches. Gather dry grass and leaves, twigs and branches, and sticks or logs. Put the tinder, which is the grass and leaves, under the twigs and branches, which are called kindling. Place the logs or sticks above the kindling. Make sure you leave some space between the materials. Fire needs air to burn.

Start the fire by lighting the tinder. If you don't have matches, this is the tricky part. In sunlight, you can use a piece of glass or a mirror to shine light onto the tinder. The heat should set it on fire. You can also rub a piece of dry wood against a rock. The **friction** will eventually create sparks, although your wrists and arms will get tired!

tinder

kindling

fuel

friction — the force produced when two objects rub against each other

18

You can also search cliffs and beaches for a flat rock called flint. Striking flint with a piece of steel creates sparks that can start a fire.

How to

HUNT FOR FOOD

Bugs! Snakes! Rodents! These aren't exactly the same as chicken, pork, and beef, right? But that's only because you're not used to eating them. In a survival situation, you have to eat things you'd normally never put in your mouth. First, you need to catch your food. You can usually catch bugs with your hands or a net. You can also use a net to catch small animals like rodents and lizards. Or you can trap them by digging a hole in the ground and covering it with grass and leaves. Place food scraps on top of the leaves as bait. You can also catch small animals with a slingshot made of cord and a piece of leather or cloth.

GO FISH

spear

Fish are an excellent island food source. If you don't have fishing equipment, you can make hooks out of wire, wood, or animal bones. Make a pole out of a long stick and string. A spear is another fish-catching tool. Attach a knife or sharp stone to a long stick or branch. Use it to jab fish that swim near you.

You can even trap fish. Pay attention to how far the high tide creeps in on your beach. When the tide is low, set up a ring of large rocks in an area that will be covered in water when the tide returns. Leave no spaces between the rocks. The next day, after the high tide has rolled back, you may find fish trapped in the rocks.

TIP: When the weather is hot and sunny, fish are often in cool, deep water. When the temperature is cold, fish usually gather in shallow, warmer water.

How to

PREPARE YOUR FOOD

You can eat animals raw if you have to, but it's much safer and tastier to cook them. For insects, pluck away the legs, wings and antennae. Boil or roast and enjoy.

Larger creatures, like birds, mammals, and reptiles, require a little more work. You'll need to slit open the body in a soft area like the belly and remove the guts. Pluck off the feathers of a bird or peel away the skin of a mammal so that you're left with mostly bone and muscle.

A spit holds roasting food over the fire.

TIP: Don't prepare your food right outside your shelter. The smell of food cooking will bring wild animals straight to your campsite.

SURVIVOR

Since 2000, TV fans in North America have seen what living on a deserted island might be like. The show *Survivor* sends a group of people to a faraway location, often an island. Though camera crews are around them all the time, the survivors live as if they are alone. They have to find their own food and water and build their own shelters. They form teams, or "tribes," to compete in races and other challenges of skill. After every challenge, one of the contestants is voted off the island. The last survivor wins a prize of $1 million.

One season of *Survivor* took place on the Cook Islands in the South Pacific Ocean.

GET OUT OF QUICKSAND

It's smart to carry a pole or stick when you're walking on an island. Use it to poke the ground in front of you to make sure you don't step into quicksand. Quicksand is sand with water flowing underneath. If you step into quicksand, you will begin to sink.

To get out of this sticky situation, don't struggle. That will only make it harder to get out. Position yourself so that you're lying on your back as close as possible to the surface. If you have a pole, put it underneath your back, either along your spine or at a 90-degree angle under your hips. Once you're floating on the surface, slowly move toward solid ground. Be patient — it can take several hours to free yourself.

How to

TREAT A BITE

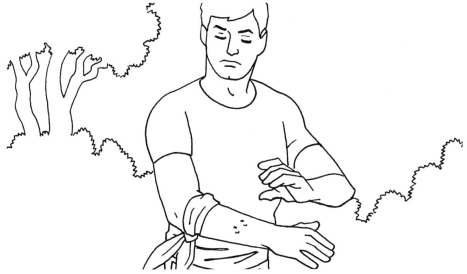

Snakes, spiders, and scorpions rarely attack humans on purpose. Rather, they bite or sting when they feel threatened. Unfortunately, many of these creatures inject **venom** with their bites. If you're bitten, wash the wound with soap, if you have it. Position your body in a way so that the bite is below your heart. This will help stop the venom from flowing through your body. Wrap a bandage about 2 to 4 inches (5 to 10 centimeters) above the bite. Make sure it's not too tight. You don't want to cut off your blood flow. Don't try to suck out the venom. It will enter any sores or openings you have in your mouth.

venom – a poisonous liquid produced by some snakes and bugs

How to

CALL FOR HELP

Two of the best tools you can have on an island are a two-way radio and a flashlight. One of the worst mistakes you can make is using them too much. Once the batteries wear out, the devices are useless.

If you have a radio, switch it on at different parts of the island to see where you get clear reception. You'll probably have to try different channels, or frequencies, before finding one that's in use.

When a plane flies overhead, switch on your radio and scan the channels for voices. If it's dark, beam a flashlight into the sky and give the SOS signal for distress. Click the light on and off three times quickly, followed by three times slowly, and then three times quickly again.

You can also use large rocks or branches to spell a word like "HELP" or "SOS." Leave your message in a clear, open area. A beach may work, but make sure high tides won't wash your message away.

Signal fires also let rescuers know that you need help. Your fire should be as strong and smoky as possible. Burning fresher wood or rubber tires that may have washed up on shore will produce extra smoke. Another option is to build three small fires in the shape of a triangle. Fires in this shape are a universally recognized distress signal.

TALKING
BY RADIO

Even if you connect with someone by radio, the person may not speak English. Here are some words that are understood around the world:

"Mayday" = "Help"

"Roger" = "Understood"

"OK" = "Yes"

People also use the military alphabet to spell out important words on the radio. For example, if you were trying to say "Hawaii," you would spell it out: "hotel, alpha, whiskey, alpha, India, India."

MILITARY ALPHABET

A = alpha	I = India	R = Romeo
B = bravo	J = Juliet	S = sierra
C = Charlie	K = kilo	T = tango
D = delta	L = Lima	U = uniform
E = echo	M = Mike	V = victor
F = foxtrot	N = November	W = whiskey
G = golf	O = Oscar	X = x-ray
H = hotel	P = papa	Y = Yankee
	Q = Quebec	Z = Zulu

CHOOSING TO SURVIVE

A little knowledge and a lot of courage can help you live on an island for a long time. Use your surroundings and the tips in this book to stay healthy and comfortable. That way, when help finally arrives, you'll be ready.

Glossary

condense (kuhn-DENS) — to change from gas to liquid; water vapor condenses into liquid water.

distress signal (di-STRES SIG-nuhl) — a call for help

evaporate (i-VA-puh-rayt) — to change from a liquid into a gas

friction (FRIK-shuhn) — the force produced when two objects rub against each other

insulation (in-suh-LAY-shun) — a material that stops heat, sound, or cold from entering or escaping

solar (SOH-lur) — to do with the sun

spit (SPIT) — a long, pointed rod that holds food over a fire for cooking

tarp (TARP) — a heavy, waterproof covering

venom (VEN-uhm) — a poisonous liquid produced by some snakes and bugs

Read More

O'Shei, Tim. *The World's Most Amazing Survival Stories.* World's Top Tens. Mankato, Minn.: Capstone Press, 2007.

Porterfield, Jason. *Shipwreck: True Stories of Survival.* Survivor Stories. New York: Rosen, 2006.

Riley, Peter D. *Survivor's Science on an Island.* Survivor's Science. Chicago: Raintree, 2004.

Internet Sites

FactHound offers a safe, fun way to find educator-approved Internet sites related to this book.

Here's what you do:

1. Visit *www.facthound.com*
2. Choose your grade level.
3. Begin your search.

This book's ID number is 9781429622820.

FactHound will fetch the best sites for you!

Index